The Eye Like a Strange Balloon

The Eye Like a Strange Balloon
Poems by **Mary Jo Bang**

Grove Press
New York

Published simultaneously in Canada
Printed in the United States of America

FIRST EDITION

Library of Congress Cataloging-in-Publication Data
Bang, Mary Jo.
   The eye like a strange balloon : poems / Mary Jo Bang.
     p. cm.
   ISBN 0-8021-4157-9
   I. Title.
   PS3552.A47546E94   2004
   811'.54—dc22   2004054432

Designed by Bart Crosby, Crosby Associates

Grove Press
841 Broadway
New York, NY 10003

04 05 06 07 08 10 9 8 7 6 5 4 3 2 1

Acknowledgments

With affection, and thanks for inspiration and encouragement, to the dedicatees below and to the following—Mark Bibbins, Richard Howard, Lynn Melnick, Holly and Eddie Silva, Susan Wheeler, and Mark Wunderlich. And my mother, Helen Simons.

"Catastrophe Theory II" is for Timothy Donnelly; "Cursive Landscape" is for Richard Greenfield; "From the Mouth of Architecture" is for Leslie Laskey; "Machine Dance" is for Marjorie Perloff; "Spots" is for Frank Schweiger; "Max Ernst and Dorothea Tanning" is for Dorothea Tanning; "Three Trees" is for Michael Van Hook.

Immense gratitude to Washington University for travel funds and the singular luxury of a sabbatical leave, as well as untold other forms of support.

Thanks to the following artists for their titles and artwork (a detailed list of which is at the back of the book): Bruce Pearson, David Lynch, Neo Rauch, Michael Van Hook, Lisa Cholodenko, Doris Salcedo, Gilbert and George, Damien Hirst, Ken Warneke, Paula Rego, Shiro Kuramata, Robert Gober, Dorothea Tanning, Victor Burgin, Cindy Sherman, Jasper Johns, Eikoh Hosoe, and Irving Penn. And to those no longer alive but whose art stands in for them: Felix Gonzalez-Torres, Derek Jarman, Elizabeth Welch, Philip Guston, Jean Dubuffet, Willem de Kooning, Ad Reinhardt, Max Beckmann, Francis Bacon, Salvador Dalí, Margaret Bourke-White, Pablo Picasso, Max Ernst, Hans Arp, and Odilon Redon.

And special thanks to Sigmar Polke, whose amazing paintings first provoked me into ekphrasis and kept me there for a very long time.

And more thanks to Timothy Donnelly.

And thanks to the editors of the magazines where some of these poems appeared, often in previous incarnations: *Boulevard, The Butcher Shop, Common Knowledge, Conduit, Crowd, Denver Quarterly, Hotel Amerika, Indiana Review, Jacket, Five Finger Review, The Germ, The New Review of Literature, The Paris Review, Pequod and Pleiades, Ploughshares, Salt, TriQuarterly, Teachers & Writers Magazine, and Mississippi Review.*

"Mrs. Autumn and Her Two Daughters" was printed as a broadside by the Dia Arts Foundation; "It's Always Been Like This" was printed as a broadside by the Underwood Poetry Foundation.

"The Eye Like a Strange Balloon Mounts Toward Infinity" appeared in *Best American Poetry* 2004 (Lyn Hejinian, guest editor; David Lehman, series editor).

The italicized lines in "The Bridge (Or, Ophelia)" are taken from James Joyce's *Giacomo Joyce.*

For Monica de la Torre

(and forever for Michael and Rusty)

Contents

Rock and Roll Is Dead, The Novel Is Dead, God Is Dead, Painting Is Dead

Only a remnant of life
left in the ill-fated confines
of the animal cage where
the Eden weasel languidly wheels
and eats what Eden weasels eat.

The cause of its pallor is called Almost
or, Almost plus Over.
And over there,
from the iceberg, you can see
any number of active disasters,

each with its own way
of unraveling
into further catastrophe.
And here are people.
They invent allegories

for private mythologies.
In their off hours, they conjure
up Alice who pours tea for eternity.
Each intimate other coexists
in the service of a different fantasy.

Miss Emma Everything walks off
and the screen fades. This?
It's a picture of a monument,
the kind where a docent can point
to where on the brick,

when the light is just right,
the insightful can see a face,
a fantastic facade.
I think there's something touching
in the hint of harmony

the architecture breathes.
In a corner, a cornice claims, Art
is the depth of whatever has deepened
an abbreviate existence.
And here is cold nature unfolding

its paramecium of pond fame.
Nothing more, nor less,
than a transient action.
How long? Yes, that's the question.
Experience returns as memory.

Scents trigger a madeleine moment.
Of course such a thing can't be hung
on the wall or sung to or sent
under a lens. Can it?
It might be here where we wish

we knew more about chemistry.
Or better, anatomy.
Page 90, "a serious thoughtful
additional effort should produce
new descriptions which would be well

worthwhile." Marks are additive
to the end where all we're left with
is the inferior olive.
Relations of long tracts
in model of medulla and midbrain.

The manual of course is important
when considering the brain.
The intelligent remove (art is text)
is the distance we desire.
The doll in the vent case

would sing if he could but he can't.
His head lists toward a smidgen of dirge
plus a ringing staccato guitar riff.
What is both an epitaph
holder and e.g. Mick Jagger? Five letters.

It's found in the corner store.
And in now sleep tight.
The coroner is still
awake, forgotten like an umbrella.
He wishes for wealth and dreams

of a call that will come
at two fifty-nine to tell him the name
of the winner of the race at three-o-eight.
And barring that,
he would just like to escape

the humdrum monochrome
of an empty world.
A skateboard flip at the end
and we're over the lip.
Pull up the moon

and pull down the covers.
We're in this season's floral print
jammies and feeling very sleepy.
Turn on the machine
that muffles the ghosts that waft

between the mind's synaptic clefts.
Beyond the classic blank
of the clear-cut
the twin movement of wind
and snowflakes is busy

embellishing the stonework.
Sing with me, won't you, please,
the entirety
of "Breathe Deep, Breathe Deep, the Divine
Breath of Irony."

Mulholland Drive

A cliché background. The mocking
of history. An aping life.
The result arrested.
She finds herself thinking
of detective stories

in which the lesson appears ridiculous
in a conceptual state.
Logic suggested
that art should exaggerate.
Uncanny strangeness

in which the "ridiculous" is nothing
less than nature.
The act of watching
The now. At the sight we are
human. A double product,

human and meaning.
The eyes of each is different.
In a classic projection of other
people's truth, each is equipped
to figure out clues.

The narrative coexists
with certitude for just a few seconds.
The characters play games
in a circle at some remove
from the world. And here,

a red herring, a cigarette aglow
in bungalow moonlight.
The heroine ought to sense something.
Someone sings a fabled "Crying Over
You." Someone cries.

Put in, with precaution, ambiguity
and uncertainty in the half-light
of a shadow. A dark road.
A slo-mo limo gravel crunch moment.
The femme fatale there,

entangled with the plot.
A world of shades and girlie Cindy
Shermans. No more mortal
electric impulse linking imperatives.
What happens disappears—or

is the past's sepia slip-on.
Caught eye, small world, flashback
casting shadows.
Evening is falling
off. The Present terminates after all

in the light illuminating the dark
melodrama enactment
of an underworld good and evil
universe where no one is certain.
The object is conscious

awareness. The fictional enacted
in syntax moves
from observation to flat state:
The car disappears and the woman is
what she is thinking.

Tact

Of course it's work, this world, this
Hydra hugging a Hercules leg. This
party of two with its tract
lawn background. Two at the velvet
rope of retraction. Skaters in blue
circling the owl eye round of an endless ring.

The curtains pulled back,
the audience is rapt.
The patterned drapes frame
the picture window then flare
into a mountainous molehill
covered with chasms and rivulets.

The metronome fans each
menacing moment.
And here's the politesse apparatus.
The stage is shallow,
later lying fallow.
The striped balloon lets go

its lampoonery air,
the air forms a cosmic container:
BAM, BLAST, POW. A spaceship takeoff.
Wheels, pulleys, a pointer
in the hand of one without sight.
It's night outside. In here,

we're as safe as this *this*
(does it hiss?) waiting to roll forward
on wheels. The rug doing nothing
like the keyboard that's missing
two hands. Below us, a ravine.
Can feelings be seen?

No, but still, we sense
the object will fall while the two remain
silent and subjugated to the drone
of the drama unfolding. To hazard
a guess. To live with hazard.
To yield to caprice. Monday,

Tuesday, Wednesday, Thursday,
Friday and pausing. Thus time passes.
She said, In an earthquake
the earth rolls. An inimitable method.
The flaw so deep
the surface adjusts rather well.

Three Trees

The aqua green goes with the pink
in a way no one knows what will happen.
Every step is a dangerous taking.
Amazing the time span of a trunk
(a door opens in it and suddenly,
someone is asking how this came to be).
The green curtain is a pressed chime
which when rung rings in a dogwood
white as if a storm were approaching
its green extreme.

Brick crumbles into living pond particle
while a bent hook holds back
the last dissolve.
An uneasy leap over a sharky sea.
Gravity plays its little emotive role.
It's Elm Street all over
again, ragged walkways lead to Toon Town.
Hello kids. Hello Jimmy Neutron.
The blanket rises, and under it,
a fetishistic pompadour

green, greener and paler than bluebird.
But hush, the nuclear power plant
is about to blow unless
Jimmy can locate the elusive button.
A siren and standing-by fire truck.
It looks like a lost cause until presto,
a messenger. A racketing aside.
The day is dragged here and there but still
can't be saved. BAM. Immediately
the next second clicks into the skyscape

apocalypse. In the dust, a celluloid woman
mows a multilayered lawn.
The arch overhead reads, O Art
Still Has Truth Take Refuge. Where? There.
There, there, says someone.

High Art

There's a city outside
the mind. Another inside.
A mind full of something
becoming because.
A face too small for this red mouth. Look how

the line isn't a street anymore
but a track. Like that. The graveled
shroud of a train. I'm not usually like
this. A linkable Like arrives without its What.
Parks the car.

I remember the camera.
The clear click. The clean cutting off
of the instant. Good-bye, good-bye.
The slide in the sleeve.
This opening eye. Wanting to take

everything in, sequence after sequence.
The framed now that never ends ending;
the blue suit pulled from a pool
of aqua dreaming.
Not knowing why aside

from theory. Sexual configurations
of glamour. What is the scene?
What is the cover? The frozen waiting
for focus and drive.
Look, look, look. Art is what

looking takes you to. A red mouth
opening to say,
Don't look away.
I'm not usually like this.
The camera sliding by with its aperture

open. Form, repetition, constructs,
content, it happens. Here is the needle
that speeds the plot to the ambush.
It happens. The Whole Truth shading desire.
Atmospherics predominating

over drama. Chiaroscuro focused
on a point of desperation.
The recurrent dream of a catalog
of surprise revelations.
Having makes wanting

continue a darkness both familiar
and strange.
"What have you got there?"
"A translation of a story of a dream
world." The sequence of events exists.

Here, one; here two;
here, buckle; here shoe.
Now let there be sound.
Now let there be light.
Once there was this now.

How Did the Monkeys Get into My Work? (Or, Table Turning)

She sat her purse down on the kidney-shaped coffee table,
turned on the floor lamp, and called
the monkey over to have a chat.
What had he done
today? she wanted to know.

He had climbed the palm tree,
he said. She knew this wasn't true
but didn't press the point.
Late night he would—arm around her neck—admit
he had trampled the snowdrops.

He had chewed on his tail.
He had mindlessly compiled pictures of flamingos
cut from magazine pages
and fashioned them into an enormous collage.
He had had it framed.

He had taken slides.
He had submitted them for review at an upstart gallery.
The curve of his tail made an S-shape
as he slid from the sofa.
Sulking now he said, See

what you've done?
And she did see. And together they sobbed.

The Three Lies of Painting

The moon as meringue.
The lancet as actual.
A dab of blood falls in the fever hospital.

The life-sized anatomical atlas reveals,
just as you'd expect, the artery as progeny,
the body as a cat circling itself,

delivering a matte mouse daily.
The tree had been torn apart
at the top by soot sifting its precious cargo

downward. Was it night? It was.
The dark of the mixed bark,
the dogs from the gulch growling

deep in their throats. Fearsome.
The heart's haunting reverberation
sending its ribboned finery homeward.

The ribcage captive to its place.
Water is weak and we separate easily.
Put your hand here. And here and here.

The tree grows in green.
The screen is a scrim.
The rock is a porous excuse

for the fact that not all is all right.
Smoking again. Rereading a child-
hood novel. Walking around a corner

only to become unglued, uncombed.
Repetition is sometimes a result
of shortsightedness. Leaning into the mirror

all they could say was: we are never
as should be but somehow we are,
clean as a freshly wiped Off.

A hand is felt moving across an age.
One, two,
three, a baby bounces on a knee. I am real

in spite of this curtain of terms.
How can that be?
Because there is that substance

into which can be added light
of any color. There is that box
into which we are drawn.

Rococo

Determined to make mischief
she took up the old operatic tradition:
sensation, color, and vain endeavor.
Dissonant interval, overwhelming effect.
Romantic dramatic she called it,

placing the action
under a canopy plumed with feathers
collected from fallen flamingos fed mistakenly
on a mixture of brine shrimp and
Frozen Shrimp paint chips.

Skaters and choirboys,
playwrights and painters—
To which, romantic dramatic, she added
five hundred fiends making the syncopated
motions of a mechanical Hellmouth

and the Y of a whale's tail.
Such was the attention to detail, that when
a hornet's nest was derided
as a travesty of excess,
a man was brought in and given a stick

with which to unhitch it and down,
down, down, it fell. Throughout all this—
fair and faithful to form—she remained fixed
to the ultimate effect of restraint,
without which, she said,

there would be no opera at all.
In the morning, she wore the Queen's costume,
in the afternoon, she played Alice
singing a flawed libretto of ludicrous lines
culminating in the musical question, Am I

only a girl in a rabbit warren?
The finale was always
when the shrapnel points of the show descended
into darkness, after which the hollow
descended dark

resulted in the hint of hallucination
brought on by a haunt of wire
strung between two yew trees
the blind boy used to use—back and forth,
back and forth. The limited possibility

pavilion on the hill playing host to it all—
the stripped hill sliding down belly first below it.

Atrabiliarios (Melancholy)

       Now they suture
the shoes in place behind vellum.
Time silent as a marble
boxed body. There's the where
and there's the coffin.
From one to the other
is a flat line and a surgical thread
mark to indicate this
distance. Sob. Someone's tears.
I do not want to be a ghost.
The beauty of it all is it's over.
Follow this, the line says and then
comes to an end. It's as easy
to ignore as hanging mist
in damp trees. Or the photograph
of a woman cut in two. The saw.
The seen. In her card stock
backing beige silk. Her red leather

shoes with an eyelet edge. Now
they suture the shoes
in place behind vellum.
The missing letters caught
in the absent text. A net.
A set question: *Where am I?*
Her shoes were found by the side of a river.

Now they suture the shoes in place
behind vellum. The sharp stab.
Creation is moving
past fast. Past the scared
feverish shivery gawking
at absence. Absence as
ice in a winter white river. Achoo.
A shoe. Oral echolalia.
Here. Hear. A multipurpose
needle just having been pushed
past the border of the skin. A cry.
Eyes in a state of perpetual
wondering until the slow crawl
comes to a halt at the edge
of the fact contraption collapse.

The Singing Sculpture

Then there's the famous
four-color conundrum of maps.
The slippery conjecture: if such
and such is true for the number n,
then it is also true for $n + 1$.

But enough. Look, Hon, how
the Champagne bubbles rise
to the top without stop.
Dawn comes yellow and dusk blue.
Uncle Andy's ankle. Underneath the arches,

I dream my dreams away.
Uncle Andy's ankle.
I dream my dreams away.
The camera captures
the submissive self, submissive

as ever. Staccato as ever.
A razor sweep cancels
the sound track. Wot a piddy.
To be human is to adhere
to the old spinal ridge division.

A dotted line determinate.
Over there is thinking; over there
is feeling. Cathexis
in the waking state lessening the insistent I.
Me minus that little test of a violent self:

H-T is bat, hat, hit, or hut.
It is hot underneath the arches.
I dream my dreams away.
A thumb snug in its bun of mythology.
The everyday fabulized.

In a painting,
a tree weeps over an arcade.
A hand opens
a curtain, please return to your seat
and sit there, looking pretty as a picture.

Everything is a preparatory drawing
for the film version
including the three sheep
in the shop window.
Shutters throw open and out

pops a head. A beautiful castle
background. Underneath the arches,
I dream my dreams
away. Après plusieurs années
(after several years).

The yellow beacon
at the center of a chaos,
touches the radium remainder. Lights,
salt, fat, flesh, and forms
fall into line.

The Magic Lantern

She admits before this she was ever
at the midnight
of not nearly ready. And even now,
there's no window
through which she can't see
the state of a future dissolve—

a wake folding over,
nicely is under.
Somewhere, but not here, not yet, she says,
something terrible is time bound to be.
(Violin verge of acrid despair.)
The view rakes in the valley, the vineyard,

the small veranda.
Rakes in the baby swallowing blue in the face
at a neighboring table its thumb.
We are halfway to dead, she says.
The amaryllis turns
to say good-bye. Enormous sky page.

Harmony behind.
The player unreeling.
And inquiry comes in. Who are you?
The king stands by his swan sled,
the cat by its cat mask.
The sound of a collision, a medium BAM,

and the music begins again. Is everything
all right? It was—
on the plate that was facing, the pumice
of nothing, slate blank and begging to be—
the vineyard moving back to the vine,
the crash to the slip.

The slope to the road. The outbreath
to its intake. This is the ache
and danger of damage, she says.
Lying there always is the you
and the you is acting
contrary to what is wise.

Mrs. Autumn and Her Two Daughters

We live in an ocean
of white waiting to fall.
One of us is not like our mother and it's me. It's I.
My eyes are mostly closed.

My mother knows
how to make snow. We never see
our feet. Our skirts end in the oncoming frost.
My sister wears ermine. I have a narrow waist.

I no longer curl my hair. Why bother?
I love my sister but hate my mother
yet we're all of a piece.
Endless snipsnip. Ragged fragment.

We still live where you last left us—
between the palace where you keep your winter
and the summer garden of the ersatz emperor.
Did I hear you say China? If I did you are right.

We live atop the continent
that contains such poverty. Such pollution.
Such eerie beauty. Always a mountain.
Always a screen. White washes

over me. I do not act
like my mother. I lean farther.
What I make annihilates the mirror of China
but not the mountain.

Not the man walking away.
My mother says throw more snow but I can't
help thinking.
There is more to being than erasure.

You are wrong she says. You don't wear your cape.

The Physical Impossibility of Death in the Mind of Someone Living (Or, Advanced Tools)

Another nightmare
in which an antigravity theory falls
off the bell tower and looks for all the world
like a limp Kim Novak in *Vertigo*.

A thriving scene and was seen turned lifeless,
ice forming inside through subduction
(theory becoming just a thing that can be stuffed
under the front seat and off one goes).

Soon a new batch of water-loving compounds
was seeking out the region
around the cathedral;
automated banking arrived at the center

of the next town over; and all the while,
we were sitting in a blended field
where land mines clenched their teeth
and waited to break new ground.

Wasn't that science's ultimate dream?
That, and to own a trompe l'oeil envelope
full of molecules self-assembling
like an opera of bodies packed

side by side on a beach
forming a slick surface over which—
Oh, a kingdom, we said, for a microscope.
For the nothing that can't be seen.

The End (Or, The Falling Out)

She loved the lyric lines that formed the house.
The sure and sharp roof, the gable diminutive,
the window breakable and sad
that way, like the fall of hair dripping
down the side of a face.

The rain sounded small
on glass as through a pane a man's outstretched arms
as if to say, What can be done
about anything now? It was ivy
up the wall and down the rain came.

The inhale of a smoky now.
The stairway narrowing, footfall by footfall
until the top, where opening
onto vista and short breathed,
the rain harder now.

That was love, wasn't it? A wind
and its wuther. Rain refreshing
the eye. And pretty sentences,
all red and green, like ribbons they fell—
dropped over a knee, draped over an arm, fell

onto the floor at their feet.
They would be buried soon
if they sat there too long.
The grosgrained grammar of them,
the rough stutter

of indrawn air, the satin surface
of a slip over which the last sentence slid
and fell. She closed her eyes
and the street gave way. The rain a heady descent,
cars weaving between trees. The petty

activity never ceasing.
The choir indicative of the symphony. Splendid.
Remarkable. Knowledge a hill.
Kneeling to bury a bird in the backyard,
the soil cold and

the played card a spade. You are means to look
at the subject. She looks instead
at the lines that form an angle steep in its wanting
rain to roll off. She reaches
up to push a cloud away and isn't able

to do any such thing. She is painted
in place. Head tilted to a shoulder, the kissed
clouds, a red car turning at the sign
of a paused moment.
The facade reorganized. Behind which

a million angles of incidence.
Each window an opening
between sutures. Everything falling out.
The harbored and hindsighted.
The symbolic and sorry.

The Tyranny of Everyday Life

The soft voice modulated to soothe.
The hair parted to studied perfection.
A step is heard
and a foot enters the ear
and a flash branches in a red laver brain.

Laughter brushes the anticubital fossa
of a bent arm a burnished head
is buried in.
And yet, the angle is reconnaissance car.
The hand is manicured.

What's behind that drape?
Busy, busy, busy.
The hive is all alive.
There's a danger sign on the side.
Mr. Mouse, come back from that edge,

says Alice, or soon we will all be over.
What does an animal live on?
she wonders. Here comes a cat. Look at that.
And here is a bed, let's lie down.
Here is a light. Here is the dark.

Stand up, sit down
like LittleMissPriss. Do you want a bit
of sweetness? Or nothing? What a trap.
In every barred box there is a bonbon.
In the ear, a head-vexing mouse squeak.

Eek equals edge. But wait, there's hope.
A forged mouse is not a real mouse.
It's made of iron. An iron is a sign
that says, I must press my dress.
And now another story, Once there was a next.

Children's Games

Let's play the game
of ruthless simplification
where we wake and say, Once

more, a great beginning.
Each morning we look
in the trinket tank and say,

The spiders look like little Jacks.
Oasis metamorphosis.
The mind will think,

will it not? Become a canvas.
There is no avoiding that.
A blade of grass. The idea of a bird, a beak.

Bones with the right amount of air?
We have flight. What can't be achieved?
But it's not free.

Ridiculous, isn't it? Sunning ourselves
on the beach of Key Biscayne.
Do you love the sound?

The Babylon of lean slab forms.
A piece of paper blows
against the fence behind

an ivy-shaped bench.
Inside the eye, it's little
more than a splinter.

A Swiss circle swims
into view, then rises canonical.
The bite of the apple—

It's delicioso, yet . . . oddly disturbing.
Irises bloom. Hello, here's rust.
There's History

collapsed into snippets
of the Battle of Hastings,
complete with calamitous sound effects.

In the Garden

We're all there. Kiki has her dog, her kitty.
And I who love monkeys have only the lion.
I wear a hat and my several hearts
all live on cactus. Kiki wears pearls
and that's as it should be. Life goes on, slipshod
or unshoed. So many scenes and all I can do is look out.
All I can do is seek shade as if sun were the worst
that could happen. As if light were a symbol
of knowing. It's not. Beautiful Kiki, her googly eyes.
Beautiful monkey, his sleek silvered forehead.
I wear red flowers that have fallen from never,
flattened to leaflings. There is sometimes silence
and sometimes sea sounds battering the edge
of my dress. Here we are and we're doing the best
that we can, this side of passive at the center of patience.
That is the game that we play.
That's the exchange—sun for shade, knowing for not.
I am even. We are posing. We are poised.
This is where we live. We are ever
but only when ever is all that there is.

How High the Moon

Is that a clock?
From this angle I can't see anything
of what's happened. Can only hear
a sullen buzz of electricity,
a gnat wishing it were, as it were,
in the tan beyond.

A pinchwork of skin is registering
an evil tick. Eyes are sighing,
sad and sad. While serious
things are happening outside.
In here two are sitting
on the How High the Moon Chairs.

Minute to minute each gives the other
a consoling smooch. It's true, isn't it,
that Time doesn't much exist.
Only art. Only x
solving itself stutteringly like a ripe balloon
on the downswing.

Unhurried love shimmies
across slick marble walls.
Upstairs, fistfuls of miniature bamboo
grow becoming all slowly.
An ear to the earth bed can hear them
as clouds form above

from cluster bombs dropped on a distant day.
In 2020 the moon will again perform full.
Fueled by reflection, by transference.
In the Sierras it's snowing.
Will we ever be less blind?
Nineteen eyeblinks, and no, and no.

Three Parts of an X

Of course I'm afraid
you won't understand.
You, a great artificial monster.
Me, a state of nature.
Rules for daily living help
only a little.

But never enough.
There are those who believe
there is an "out there."
Which can make a problem
seem smaller, like a nickel
in the hand of man standing

in the corner of a casino.
Outside in the garden, a man
sits looking up. He's thinking,
In spring, when woods are getting green
I'll try and tell you what I mean.
Of course we are flying

blind. Of course we are frightened.
And some succeed, that's true.
Each evening they close the curtains
and watch their TVs.
Then someone says, Time
to get up, and they get.

Time to move, and they move
to place an x in the box next to naughtiness.
What harm is there in art?
As long as an image can never bed
the object it represents.
Sex with an effigy.

How much fun could that be? Tsk. Tsk.

Envy and Avarice

One wants a red sky at night.
One has two white-tipped ears,
one wants three. One, a wide tail.

They annoy equally.
Equally they bite the bone.
They are muscular. They are bad

dogs. At night they change
into leopard suits
and become troublesome.

They are all interaction.
They are all
intention. Total immersion

in the task.
Distortion by smoke and muffled mirrored sea
bottom where the seaweed waves back at her.

Distortion by wanting
what she wants. Boating down
a blue vein. Lavender escapade.

Nothing above, hierarchically speaking.
The last bird alive goes flying away.
Both biting the bone. All appetite.

Both gnawing. Arms waving and average red
avenging mouth spouting "Farther, William"
and getting it all wrong.

Spots

A pink-faced lovebird cooed from its roost.
A box had been opened, a vase broken.
And against the green wall, the sea was sliding
back again. It was a delicate landscape
of water and mist. A view of nature

derived from a book entitled *How to Find
the Cat in the Biosphere*.
The mirrors were mourning-envelopes, black
with cousinly concerns. A man came down the stairs,
brushing lint from a pant leg.

He was back from Michigan
where his tie had taken up the theme
of interlocking clowns eating ice cream.
The television was on. Someone was speaking
saying, Where did you stay?

And, Who's to say? And, Where's the violin?
Or, There's the guy named Lindh.
Somebody's badge was silver.
So was the tea set. Context is everything.
Mister Eddie Silva of Holland Park Gardens

and his charming wife, Holly, ever adorable,
if expected, in red, were two exiting
the east gate of the garden at four. They slid
from the screen. The sound of a second
through a vein. Five, and the hum of a faucet.

History, we could clearly hear
the caterpillar badgering Alice, is today's phone
ringing in a film. We didn't dare interrupt
to say we'd heard it before.
At least an hour earlier. At least as an echo

escaping a sound studio. And Art—he paused
to draw a small puff of smoke—is the murmur
of incoherence as it brushes off fact.
That, of course, was the moment
when the characters turned to face the world's terms.

Etched Murmurs (Or, The Common Green Libretto)

Two birds were singing silly.
Two books fell
        from the wooden shelf.
The pilot light produced tinny spitting
        sounds. Zoom.

She pressed her skirt and spritzed
a thin mist of water from a plastic bottle
onto the yellow. There.
        The pilot light flickered
green-blue but of course
        it couldn't be seen.
Sight divided
from seeming sound

and suffering as outside
there was vastness happening and trouble
was happening.
        Some unhappy boy
cuffed his dog. (The howl of a dog set up
        next to the mezzo-
forte of two teens with boom boxes.)
Fossil of poverty

stuck in the mind's stupid
mill.
The day conceding
        to the terrible
        morning speech
        of the *Times* smacking the stoop.
Slapping. Three minus two
shuffle down the corridor.

An endless cry—
(trilobite of sound mirrors missing
their silver lining)
          giving a hemmed-in video slit
onto someone's poor
          forgotten issue.
The sock stuffed
in the child's mouth. What

a world.
Surreptitious
puddles. Essence of borrowed
          speech, suffused throughout
with ether or ethered sleep.
          The little lyric bottom
of the grooved green moon
redeeming nothing.

Off-white shimmering
doom-kiss. Good-
nightandgoodmorning.

The Bridge (Or, Ophelia)

She should have brought a book to read—
a trim volume, a novella,
a stack of stunned swallows pressed
into paragraphs on nifty rice-paper pages.

Instead she was left watching a man
feed a silver coin to an open-mouthed meter.
She had ordered pasta with pesto and waited.
There had been pee smell in the subway apse,

ankle straps on a pair of patent pumps.
On that particular Tuesday,
she couldn't take her eyes off the wonderful
wool in the window opposite,

a bleached blue so light it might as well not be
blue but for picking up a whisp
of a slant sky hue and holding it.
Someone had been unkind last night.

Someone had said, Get thee, and Get thee.
Clearly she had mistaken fire
for some galling ember.
Will he ever come again? No, never.

Rue for you, rue for me. The small street ended
in a cul-de-sac beneath the bridge.
Above, the noise of some ecstatic blastment,
a battalion of Comemycoach

and Goodnightladies.
This mixed with the softish, silken swish
of an overhead fan.
In a rotting wooden box, Parma violets grew

heavy in scent. Hey nonny no.
A group of fresh-faced acolytes
from the Convent
of the Sacred Heart passed in front of the glass.

A faint breeze, a rippling shadow.
Her eye caught the corner
of the Queen's orchid cape
as it swept by.

A fountain threw its dilly drops
of water down.
Would he never come again? Yes, never.
Against that backscrape of sound and

the hue of illusion of the vegetable glass of nature
and of lush grass, the hair of graves,
and of some hinted and heaven-weft scent,
dressed in black taffeta, the daffodil waited.

Catastrophe Theory IV

There are multiple versions. In one,
the egg salad goes bad, in another—the baby, the bath-
water. In the more recent, running, waving arms,
poultry, and spats to conceal the absence of socks.
The socks have been held back
for puppet production.

In the most recent, the train is a choo-choo.
Benign and friendly. We know it's not so but we so wish
to believe. In this one there is also the hint
of a fence and lavender which will stand
for more than a violent resistance to reason.
It also speaks

of spilt ink but it stays
in its contour. It is, in a word, controlled.
How catastrophic can that be?
Clearly, the theory is not without mishap—
especially along the horizon.
And there are unsolved portions

in the right lower quadrant.
A place that is tender
to palpation. What you don't see, you can still feel.
You can, in a word, presume
that at the bottom of the bottomless depth,
the band will render splendidly, from sheet music

not easily found, the famous "One Fine Day"—
in which the watchtower turns
to a lifeguard beneath an unbeached umbrella
and seven geese rise from the ashes
like falcons off forth on swing, night falling
down around the waning.

Catastrophe Theory III

Now we sit and play with a tiny toy
elephant that travels a taut string.
Now we are used and use in turn
each other. Our hats unravel
and that in itself is tragic.
To be lost. To have lost. Verbs

like veritable engines pulling the train
of thought forward. The hat is over-
turned and out comes a rabbit. Out comes a man
with a monocle. Out comes a Kaiser.
Yikes, it's history, that ceiling
comprised of recessed squares, each leg a lifeline,

each lie a wife's leg. A pulled velvet cord
rings a bell and everyone comes running
to watch while a year plummets
into the countdown of an open mouth. A loop of razor wire
closes around the circumference of a shaken globe
of snow. Yellowed newsprint with its watery text,

a latticework of shadow thrown
onto the clear screen of the prison wall.
From a mere idea comes the twine
that gives totality its name. What is a theory
but a tentacle reaching for a wafer of reason.
The inevitable gap tragic. Sure, tragic.

Catastrophe Theory II

The foot goes forward, yes.
Yet there are roots. And a giant orb
which focuses its cyclopic eye
on a moiré morning.
When the microcosm is dry—it's earth;
wet—it's water.

Water, reeds, electric eel: one possibility.
Sun, reeds, dust mote and mite: another.
Whatever the elements
(it's urban/it's pastoral,
it's empty/it's open), the theory says
it could always be worse.

Until it is. Then theory fails,
leaving a tracer mark.
From blood you come to blood
you go. Sudden things happen
inside a frame. A flame is
lit. Look

at those pathetic wiggly squiggles.
Inferno or garden?
An immeasurable distance
sizzles between them.
Watching it all. But taking so little in.
Just what will fit on the flat

of a glass lens. The ticker is hopeful.
Pathetic fallacy.
Look at the numbers move.
The mystery of ticks.
One per second, sixty per Mickey.
Four becomes ten, one in six

bombs falls in a bushel, a basket,
a two o'clock casket. Do you wish to stay
connected? The seen blurs
into the just heard. A bird outside the wide
open window. The warm day
of March. It changes. It has

all changed. The world
as a distracting disaster.
MY, what little SENSE you make, said the wolf
to Mary Jo. The theory rests
on a tipping point.
The clock steps in a direction.

This Is How You Sit Correctly (After Goya)

Fathoming the essence
of a delicate fear. Ravished
by a dream of a spotlight

lighting the dying deer's face.
[For antler, see ante- plus oculus (eye).]
Her mind

was a cascade of cheap shots
from the argument that still stung.
She slipped easily out of bed

and went to work.
Bitten from the middle.
Born from the muddle.

What's admitted by the door can be kept
by the mind. Can be trapped
in a list. Can be lifted

by the tail and tenderly placed
where it will no longer be
in the way. It was never easy.

Or else, it was far too
like a banner made
with a pole and a shirt.

White works well.
How do you feel right now?
Where are you getting your information?

Do you have a belief system?
How much fear did you experience
today? I was shaking in my boots

equals five. You wave a white shirt
fastened to a pole. Be correct. Be bright.
Anything can become

an object. All-or-nothing divided
like a second erected
on a slanted slice of Time. When rules are broken,

what is correct will only be decided
after. If "h" seemed invented
to look like a chair,

"n" might come to be just an ottoman.
She looked back. He'd said, This
is the right way—

hands clasped, hand on a hand.
Feet froze to the floor.
After that, what?

The dog in its basket would bark.
The foot on the carpet would sink.
A finger would point

out a question. So sitzen sie richtig
(nach Goya). The hem of her floor-
length dress raised the tooth

of the surface, each hit of the fabric
made a wickerwork wave
until the motion became an alignment

of doors inside every which was a head
plus a hand, part of a life,
or at least half of a nebula within which

a whole constellation of stars.
She waited and watched
while the lines on the floor formed

a grid behind which a house-
ful of happy delinquents
all sleeping soundly in beds.

Going Out

Iridescence that was
no more than caught light but still we said
snake and snake it was, the serpentine

river twisting across
some cracked country fissure
after fissure until

a nexus of twin towers, a tiny bridge,
a description, its scalloped top
perfectly pretty

as a picture. Riding on
time, the two thin legs of the M mudstuck
and snow at the edges, green bleeding

through, a blend of the castle
we'd come from, the sleeping
beauties we'd been. Nota bene. The salt mine

we'd worked in.
Azalea faces florid and red-raw.
Looking down one wondered.

One boat caused a wake.
The others were sleeping.
Frail as a failure,

the friable coast was lashlike.
Good, we said, speaking
to the tiny ripples

that gave the water its texture.
We'll give them trees
green leaves in the spring.

For now, we said, we'll simply map
the marvelous monochrome. The cold
resignation of out-

waiting a winter (the particular
flowering) design
bedded in the scrape of a boot

as it crosses the Victorian footbridge.
Frozen boats floating at the center
of a pond—shapeless and navy as night.

Night hissing at the back of our necks.
Our trunks. Our black coats.
All this and more

about to be resurrected.
Each moment's death giving birth
to the reiterative need

for continuance. For what? For this:
the line played out.
Duration lasting like fireworks

in a late millennial display.
Apogee. Nadir. Particular. Flowering.
A phase. Was it possible to be less abstract?

It was. But only if—
and something kissed the moment closed.
Some broken hand of a clock,

limp and idle, unable
to tell anything. Only the mouth does that.
Only the hand. Or a scratch

at the door. The dog coming in.
The door coming in.
After witnessing a terrible crash

and now he won't be taken there anymore.
He'll lie at the door and whine
but will not be taken to.

It's Always Been Like This

Under the light the line on probability read,
"Each letter tends to be unlike the foregoing
letter." Then how to explain,
"The bride looks too good"?

Against tendency,
she guessed. She saw eyes down
demurely, eyes
to the right. Pearls grounded in patience.

After that, a somnambulant catalytic
would stir in lethargy and get back inaction.
She had woken once with sleep
in the eye, crawled from beneath

a moment of hoarseness
just as
The Committee for a Reasonable World
was being called to order. Was ordering,

Put T in a pan and heat it. What did T equal?
In the paper, a directive caption: Look at me.
To the right a neighborhood;
to the left a neighborhood.

A shutter of guises each reading itself,
each knitting itself a numeral.
How songlike. How singular. However
no one was more than one. No matter how many.

Untitled #70 (Or, The Question of Remains)

The day she put on her glitz teardrops
and O Hon lip gloss,
ate an orange on an empty
and took the 8-train
to Grackleville, she met a man
climbing a narrow stairwell,
repeating to himself, This is all, this is all.
The music of a popular march played
in his head. This, he said, is all,
directing any further comment
to a longtime opposition blooming in his chest.
No, he said, to the offer
of a chaotic labyrinth of clouds,
devotion, rain, creatures of fables,
and opulent solitude.
Alone he entered the thicket
of empty situations, the rhetorical force
of conversation,
muttering as he went, This is all—

Apprentice to death. Toxic grace.
Terrible and beautiful repose.
Dismay and murkiest waters.
The blighted morning.
The coordinate night.
The sad fact of the pink glow
of Grackleville's late iridescence.

The Tempest (Or, Don't Know Why There's No Sun Up in the Sky, Stormy Weather)

The urge to see through things.
The day begins with a shimmer,
the blue square becomes a window, the box
a building. The vertical lines the final
page in an exercise book that's closing
over last year's profusion of lilacs.
By the banks of the Mississippi, she sat down
and wept. The rapture was over.
Now a melding of comic motifs
with tragic. The knife on the balustrade
did not bode well. She lay down
in a green sweater, rested
the back of her hand on her forehead.
The private acts become strange
when subjected to inquiry.

You get on a bus.
The bus takes off
from the base of a column.
There is singing somewhere. Then you're sitting
on a mohair sofa. Smoking the last cigarette
that must last a lifetime. In a red dress
you answer a telephone
and say,
so sweetly, I.

Allegory

Let us console you.
Music's the answer.
Of course, we're caught
in this sphere
where it doesn't much matter

whether our song reaches
the ear of Prometheus or not.
He's adamantly chained
to the mountaintop.
Every morning, there's eagle,

a beak and a claw on the back.
Such an ache. Somatognosis
is the sixth sense.
What does it feel like
to inch one's way forward?

These are the questions.
Dawn on its knees
crawls toward knowledge.
More of us are coming.
All of the adoring.

Every day is another broken
tie on a red-leather shoe. A Who-
do-you-wish-to-be?
Tonight we'll be content
with whomever we think we are.

The door of the car will click-close
and off we'll go.
In the back is the Jackself
we might have been.
What's the degree of remove

between the one at the top
of Pie Mountain
and the tourist motel
at the bottom with its pool
of aqua attitude and blue inflatables?

Some vigorous enactment.
Is it three o'clock or twelve fifteen?
Either is only an estimate.
Myth equals fate
plus embellishment.

The wheel is set in motion
when our eyes are on the moment.
Later, we drive on four wheels
to the carnival and line up
for a ticket; the air is rife

with summer.
The kinesthetic lift of a foot
from the floor
forces itself to be felt.
The actors are standing

against a wall and watching
it all unfold. Look,
they say, at the minutiae sutured
to the spine of the climax
when somebody opens the door

on the side of despair
and looks out onto death
and destruction.

Blue Thought Circle

A statement followed by an "oh,"
perfectly equally matched to an "and."
Was it as simple as that?

And *now* what?
The clock stopped and restarted.
Chemicals coursed

through a bloodstream
slowly pouring a pitcher
of bright yellow. Astonishingly

beautiful that yellow
sun brightening each sky,
surviving the leveling of each worn moment.

Yet remaining spotlessly new,
with shiny chrome trim;
a long line of taxis matched it.

A vivid image, vividly recalled
upon waking. Like Art.
Or,

the world called a tray
on which one carried
the surface of a deadpan face

into the bathroom and washed it.
And held a warm cloth,
then took a small square

of gauze, a prepackaged solution,
and gently rubbed
back and forth slowly erasing the eyes,

the nose, the messy mouth.
Always afraid
of monotony. Make that metonomy.

Cursive Landscape

In the reverse psychology of earnestness, more
suddenly meant less. Every tear was a crocodile
hanging from the underlid.
Every nose had its neat dot of moisture.
And for wisdom, there was the Dalai Lama.

Who would have thought that a sensible scheme
put down in print would be more sensible yet?
In the sharpened districts where we lived we lived
our little lives, skating on the flat tops
of torn tree trunks divided from root.

What little ledges.
What arrogance was required for each inbreath.
We were offended by the vaguer terms: something,
anywhere, every. Nothing. By the vaguer scenes
seen through windows.

Lives our lives would never touch.
Everything asked. Nothing given.
The grand trees stood guard over a tan and green blank.
To each, the trees meant differently.
To one they were oranges. To another they were branches

divided into a family
frenzy. A sotted father swaying
in the height over a too-small trunk.
Children laughing up into it
with their cruel manners and mud-smeared faces.

To the last, they were color gone bad
in the late November plentiful sorrow.
Tomorrow they would be nothing. Lean-against
haven for the breathless and senseless. Houses
for the harried. Squirrels.

A dog barking at the bottom of one.
Once she saw some
uprooted. Like herself laid down into restlessness.
They were breaking her heart she said.
Leafing flattened into feeling. She felt

them falling she said. And turned.
Later we would say it was a golden age,
a dazzling epoch, and if the trees were slight
in their part it wasn't our fault. Every truth
like no other. No nothing was ever our fault.

Alice in Wonderland

Such a fall! Watch fob and waistcoat.
How late the mistake is made.
How long the clamoring lasts.

Who are *you*? Bending against a blade
of green grass. Smoke fills
the Caterpillar. Smoke floats

over the polka dot snow.
Have you really changed, do you think?
This is the best part of the dark edge of down.

Down, down, she fell. This is the best part
of the edge where one is not one-
self. Don't I know it, Alice says,

blinking her eyes once twice.
She took down a jar from one of the shelves
as she passed it; it was labeled "ORANGE

MARMALADE." The game was changing.
There are games where one never wavers.
There are games where one follows

a dot-by-dot disturbance.
There is falling, and about to
fall, and ground giving way.

There is the beautiful
act of turning
to buy two and getting a free beach bag.

Perfect for picnics or toting and such.
A flavorful favor to take on a trip
to a mountain where chocolate is eaten

on weekends and during the week
it's placed on your pillow
right next to your head which is swimming

in visions. She could almost envision it.
A pool with a placid surface,
mist shrouding a peak

that poked through at the top
to speak of impossible heights.
But, no. The peak was a spike

on the cephalogram and she was dreaming again
in a sleep-clinic bed.
Father was petting her forehead;

Mother was stirring a soup.
She'd be ever more
reckless if never she woke.

Now that was not said right.
Some of the words had got altered.
A row of button mums hedged the walkway.

She stopped
to enter this datum
in her Rite as Reign notebook.

She knew what the button mums meant.
Another fall.
Dying must happen quite often, said Alice.

Minnie Mouse

But would you love me just as much
if I had nothing at all?
Sure, Minnie, more than ever!

Of course love is a) malleable matter
of culture. And a wife
is (a wife). And what

about number eight?
Do you too see the world as formal
decisions, technique and touch?

The frenetic
as typical of lines formed "with sticks
or the end of a paintbrush, suggest[ing]

the primacy of the drawn or painted mark."
If you do, we'll be friends.
Theory reduces all that

to a sentence: A picture is little
more than its parts plus the marriage
of time to its nothing, less now.

I'm trying to think
past the edge of my own rickrack slip.
On the hill are three trees. Let's pretend

it's a picture illustrating the notion
that beauty is a bridge
trembling under today—

The insane questions that one cannot solve.
The sleuthhounds bark,
horns fanfare

the familiar. The herald announces
the weather is rainy; a drizzle conceals
the castle. A cut ribbon divides

the beginning
from some already ever after. I'm after
proof that I'm more than what can be

dismantled into small bits of ideas,
then pressed and rebuilt
as the essence of innocence.

Lovers (Or, The Tropic Bride)

What she needed was
a bird, a beak, something rock hard that could break
the crystalline cold that encased her (tap, tap, tap,

against the tin-
ny window). Pleasure a votive for memory, a motive
candle at the shrine of the one who'd refused

to be begotten. He sat looking back
over his shoulder at the building. It was crude
cathexis that had brought them there.

Did she wish, he wanted to know?
Sure she wished but—
He was covered with cat fur, a feral found

behind a stack of firewood, red feathers flecking the snow,
a mouth tasting of sacrifice. Crimson minutes. Tiny ticks
in the cat's fur removed with tweezers.

Each leaving a purpural mark. A purple trade,
this for that. Scar
for what was done to one. An impulse

to unrest the surface, the earned quietude, flitted
but then it did what it did, it fled.
Took flight. That bird at the wheel,

over the lintel bridge, while through the door
a tide. A tap turned, a flood gush sweeping
them down the hill. They sat. Stunned there.

Doll

In the dream there'd been difficulty—
tidal wave topside while elsewise
the cat had to be taken away and left yet again

on a farm framed by a row
of small houses. A tangled mass hissed and we woke
and went on and found a pay phone,

called the weather station. Wondered what
was for lunch. A starboard lurch made us wonder
again whether we'd been right all along.

I went in to take a nap
and beheld that the bed held a doll and her blanket.
Her mesh thigh-highs reminded me of *Cabaret*—

the film, not the play.
Lying there the day dissolved until
another formed fresh

and I woke facing the hill.
The hill climbed to the top
of the mountain. Was rock and a ragged moonscape.

The fate-reader had said, This
is your sylf and had pointed to a sliver
pared from the larger piece. And this—she had pointed

to the gargantuan rest—is patience, that game you play.
Little zombie of the inner eye.
Little shudder of the frighted mind.

The landscape was Siberian Birch, bark white
against blue. The fragment in the window, as always,
incomplete and perfect

as only the partial can be.
It is here I would have told her
I loved her

but couldn't. It is here, baby doll in blanket
and bed against a wall with the mountain as message,
we took the moment some call a small pleasure.

In Memory of My Feelings—Frank O'Hara

She could find reason
anywhere if she looked
for it. The clock told her
to get up. She got up.
       She ate.
The plot is the one thing we know, said Mandelstam.

Irritation gave way
to something else. The mind
as a well-organized cabinet
where a spoon and a fork were looking out
       of place.
Reason wasn't the hinge

on which memory swung.
A truism escapes its cage.

A bark brings you back to it. You are
who you are, the self said
       to the self who did what it wanted.
The knave was another kind of person.
Mean.
He had winter in his heart.
She could find meaning
       in the metaphor of a (   ) missing knife.
She was cold.
She reached for her coat. I've never seen anyone

like you.
The truism was true. That will do.

There was that day made of clay.
And there's each piece
of tile that makes an entire
(*clear, supple, or there*).

How many selves? he asks at the counter.
I'll take a dozen. Wrapped and sent
somewhere. Someone serves
up a plate of devils.
           Another eats them wearing a red dress
and a black beanie.

The pendulum swings
and in so doing makes a pattern.
           Each is only one.
The serpent in the middle is that vituperative viper
hiss-spittle hung from its fangs.

To be true blue is something.
The rule breaks.
The paint drips. We are all human.
We are all fork and spoon
on a string around our neck.
           Let me through. There's some pushing
aside by the diva.
In memory of the single clear moment.
Time-defined.
The glint of silver on a spoon.

Which one of your many selves is looking
into that mirror? One? All? One and all
the little dragons at the door?
        Someone reaches out and a pair of scissors
says, Snip. There go the threads
that hold us together.
Someone serves up a witchy brew when someone doesn't
        say I'm sorry.
Someone says ready.
Someone slices off a life with a missing knife.

Man and Woman

To spend most of a short life living,
that was the aim. She'd know it since
the first time her heart's hand had
painstakingly formed
its aortic scrawl, its Palmer Method
of pulse, pulse, pulse.

I love to be brought, he said,
into the city. The bread
and butter so simple, so pure.
The waiter in a long white apron cleaned
their places. Finished, he asked?
One was never.

Breakfast followed dinner.
Sleep was a wave
one rode to wake gasping.
Sea salt awash in the vein.
Cheek imprinted with sleep's ragged S.
And even prettiness could be dissolved

and reconstituted. Stone falling
from an eave could be gravel
at the base of a pylon.
A python knowledge grasping her
in its grip. Such a pretty blouse.
The sequins, the salesman had said,

had been sandblasted and no extras included
because none would be needed.
The firm was so sure they would last.
While nothing lasts, she said, still it is
for a while— He helped her
on with her coat. The blouse is black.

The pattern of tiny circles forms
a sequined paisley,
a pretty method of fragility.
I love to be brought, he said,
into a language. And so did she.
The white snapdragons,

the peach cheek, the pretty girl
in her black backless dress.
It was all dissolving
into a hangman's noose.
Into a taut track—
the caboose following the train

into the tunnel tunneled into a mountain.
The children piper-bound
following the train.
Don't open your eyes.
I have been waiting
my whole life, he said, to be brought

into believing. Practicing
with a daiquiri, dealing with timidity
in any number of ways.
Wearing a hat, driving a Lexus.
It's difficult. The black blouse,
the clear sequins, each a little lake

taking Ophelia in,
to oblivion. Into a language
that would suit her. The noise level
in the restaurant had risen.
The girl in the black dress (Ophelia?)
was wiping her eyes.

The woman in the pretty black blouse
sewn with sequins was turning
to look out the window.
Did I tell you, he said? Yes,
he had. He had told her.
And she had listened.

Abstract Painting, Blue

Why are children jealous
of their fathers? Steps
run up against the stones
which gate tombs,
flagstone oratories
where the organ murmured,
where the dead posed face.
Nothing water-bottles!

A youth carries out in leaves
a greyhound. Do they cry?
They cry I. I am not unaware.
The curious remain
a chorus. Time took a step
and said, Who expired?
Some rich person,
another right hand.

And art?
I was occupied.
Exempt at the time.
One of the monstrous figures
that sculptors attach
by the shoulders to gutters
squeaked and twisted.
I encouraged a smile.

Art gave me the first
conditions of art,
which is *idea*.
Isn't this the "here Me I exist"?
That positive orates the room.
In drama everywhere is seen,
as I see you. It is better
than the mirror.

Scissors sound from the vault and then. . . . And then? And then
the street woke up me. I had a dream. It was Saturday. What do
you want? Theory to be forced to answer the curious.

Study for a Portrait

Languor was seeping in-
to the crevice between collar and flesh.
Heads were tilting
toward and away. And everywhere ice.

He kissed her electric
in the elevator, then disappeared.
There is no logic, she said, like that
of bricks—

each one following the next across
the sight line then falling
in at the window. Silver was the light
behind him

and a bluster of metal the curtain
that closed. The sky blued by what was
beyond it, the music blurred.
Little thunder of the wasp nest

in the window corner.
Little thunder of the heart, the sulphur vein
down the side of the neck.
The falling-in kiss

in the thural light of the later day.
She knew, did she not,
that that would be the last
blessed sacrifice for all her little errors.

Masquerade

How does he love me? Not at all
or a little bit. Catbrat, he says,
leaning briefly toward me
like the wind-battered candle

in the wide open window—
it's a blinking noon on tonight.
We're here to celebrate the end
of what can't last

past dawn. Someone says, Turn
the model's head just a touch
and my head goes to the right.
Tonight, we'll turn

on some music. Turn on some music.
Turn on the stage lights.
The stage lights go up, at least a few,
and it's lovely.

I've said it before,
There's a calm kind of knowledge
in distance.
We're supposed to stay quiet.

Herr Moment here is fond of living.
I, on the other hand, am fond
of all opposites. We're holding still
perfectly. Will the weather hold?

Now they're saying it's a question
of how to train nature
to recognize evil.
We can hardly recognize ourselves.

Max Ernst and Dorothea Tanning

Listen, here, as always, there are links—
the silent stamp of a man's hand
gestures to events experienced

in a previous picture. Here, it says,
look here. But I can't turn
my head past a point. I imagine

he loves me, so he loves me.
He wears a brown outfit.
He reminds me of no one

else. Non-metaphoric.
Non-metamorphic
in the moment of taking.

He was once in a boat
with fire in his hand. Wind blew
his hair. It's enough, isn't it?

That fabric can imitate a body
of water. To be asleep
with eyes wide open.

Later, we'll dance, if dancing's allowed.
And sing a freakish song I know
you know:

"Will you, won't you, will you,
won't you, will you join the trance?"
We were beautiful as hell.

The air was impalpable there
surrounded by the impalpable
firmament.

If nice means precise,
we are.
We don't blink. We stay stopped.

Birthday

In the tight-wove of hold-on, she was caught
and would not let be go.
He had taken her thin wrist, looked her in her face and—
placed an odd wish in her ear.

She had let herself be led to the door where he stopped
telling the story; the moral was muddied
but something along the line
that want could be controlled but at what cost.

She sat silent.
An hour does stand still, he said. Here.
On the blade edge between an action
and its unflustered *-ed* ending.

The corridor was closed at one end.
At the other, a window threw itself open
to the vast milieu of metaphor—
lamp for light, tree for knowledge,

dog for no known more faithful.
Allow me, he said—
and began to describe a reversible spell,
as well as the selling of ideas

in a season on edge.
A man on a ledge tipped over and fell
to his feet. There was a draft and a sudden upswing
of wind made her feel she was nothing

but a wind-washed Winona
looking scared where she stood.
A doorman opened the door and looked in
on himself. The future was brewing. Today was

sweet knifely brief. Without afterlife
or lack. Without ambivalence or any-
thing missing. A momentum perfection—ink blot
of inwish and over. Yet unalterably was.

The Phenomenon of Ecstasy

In the brothel diorama I took the missionary position
deciding in advance that there is no under,
only equals, only parallel lines
across which will blue the onset of wonder.
>   The cat-puppet dances
>   hinge-kneed in a faint
>   light that falls through
>   an elongated slit.
With your free hand you can dial-a-season: It's October
or it's April. It's flux
of a mouth touching down on another's.
The other touches back. A cold mirror between. Dark
on the far side. Blind on the near
but for a rake of light caused by part sparkler/
part a winter mint bit in a nighttime room.
A compulsion to count.
The bare body. The heart's downbeat
assaults the spine. A slight movement to the right
and my foot makes a chair
list, blister of unbroken air at an altar of ear.
Alternatives call for too much.
Architecturally speaking, I'm a restorative friction,
the sarcophagus lid above me wearing away
at resistance. A doll on her back. On a bed
being taken apart. Look at me dying.
I am lying. I am not.

Machine Dance

As all the moons to water
                  and we obedient
in sync between two suits we sit
         we kneel we stand.

One suit of blue and one of soot
         a train racing
toward a windrowed view.
               I am a camera's rein

tracing the pause diminished
         between the shuddered
clicks. F-stopped and pushed into the now.

         We came we read we tilted
our head and all in unison.
             All for one and one
as a white shirt can be a sun

         to black. We were ballet
as now we are a map
         machine of history
holding on. Some of us are mere idea.

            We wait for break
to sweep us to a small café next door
         where waiters bring us coffees
on trays of tempered steel.

         We sit in twos and take it.
We say in French, Pour nous
and then we say, Pour more.

Physiomythological Diluvian Picture

Kaleidoscope Dan has his eyes closed.
No irritable reaching after fact and fiction.
He's the sea's reach in the season of sleeps.

The dinosaur in a Rorschach twists
his neck around to see into the future.
Reborn into civilization, he opens his eyes to look

through the window at a commotion outside.
A birdie girl is seen looking at her shoes
and watching the street with one eye.

The rain had begun so
the umbershoots black taffetas were being unfurled.
Sure, he says, from here I can see

how a flood could occur. He imagined making
matched sets of dinosaurs disembark
from a ramp that worked from the wings

via a now nearly outdated system
of elongated weights. The lion comes out
of his lair. Ticktick of a reel. Back at the bay,

a woman walks out the door. Finds the street
a warm sea, the color of the sea.
The view on the right is dark, scizzored

by lightning's visible after
canvassing straight rain with silence.
An incision is being made into the pocket

where the inner truth is hidden.
Impossible—and worse, already done—
but stillness is watching. A light winks

in the box of a window. A fire or a fork
on a table. The bow tie at the top
of the street glistens

then twists like glazed glitter. She twists around
to watch time creaking a boat at the coast.
Her drip-spattered mind is forming

a mathematical design, in-wrapped in a series
of folioed fold-ins. Convoluted fissures
named and numbered: one, two, three—

Where's Tweedledee? a gruff voice asks.
He was standing sleepy-faced facing
an elaborate arcade,

each ovoid individual arch housing its own
evidentiary Etruscan statue.
The lead was reading,

"Being had become an eye,
subjecting seeing to it." There was also a wall,
at the bottom of which was a bit of eggshell.

Les Demoiselles d'Avignon

Over here our story begins
and over there it continues
like the idle hum of the clown car.

Wot a piddy, says the Kat,
that the corporal occupies the moment.
The forever echoes.

The electroencephalograph echoes.
Someone hands you a graphic,
a penciled-in footprint

belonging to a boy named Bart. What
are we to do with this? Make it fit.
The body is now a bee carcass

floating on aqua. The self is consistent
but the story is made
of fragments, color-coded, ballooned,

or cubed. An earthquake shattering
the shaken one-point perspective.
All about is a field

of permission, of vision, a force
of ellipsis. What gives
our bare legs their persimmon tint

is intention plus Taffy Apple oil
with underdrawing. We are drawn
in. If we seem vulnerable

under the past-pattern of clouds
in motion, over a pale blue
conveyor-belt ocean, it's because we are.

Sometimes we act like we love
small Peruvian parrots.
We hide them in our hair.

The Eye Like a Strange Balloon Mounts Toward Infinity

We were going toward nothing
all along. Honing the acoustics,
heralding the instant
shifts, horizontal to vertical, particle

to plexus, morning to late,
lunch to later yet, instant to over. Done
to overdone. And all against
a pet-shop cacophony, the roof withstanding

its heavy snow load. So, winter. And still,
ambition to otherwise and a forest of wishes.
Meager the music floating over. The car
in the driveway. In the P-lot, or curbside.

A building overlooking an estuary,
inspired by a lighthouse.
Always asking, Has this this been built?
Or is it all process?

Molecular coherence, a dramatic canopy,
cafeteria din, audacious design. Or humble.
Saying, We ask only to be compared to the ant-
erior cruciate ligament. So simple. So elegant.

Animated detail, data from digital.
But of course there is also longstanding evil.
The spider speaking
to the fly, Come in, come in.

Overcoming timidity. Overlooking
consequence. Finally ending
with the future. Take comfort.
You were going nowhere. You were not alone.

You were one
of a body curled on a beach. Near sleep
on a balcony. The negative night
in a small town or part of an urban abstraction.

Looking up
at the billboard hummingbird,
its enormous beak. There's a song that goes . . .
And then the curtain drops.

From the Mouth of Architecture

On the facade, egg-and-dart meets the architrave
and in the arches, impost to impost,
the held breath
of a stopped real. Inside, she is object—

genre-bound precious in a white-walled vault.
This is how the self stays
a self, she says. Unbendingly. She tries
the glass-paneled doors plaid-wrapped

in wrought-iron sleeves, all art
deco. Locked, they served to keep her
behind herself where pictures are lashed
and alarmed, and words remain one

with their categories: plaqued, apt, or inadequate.
Each frame is a frame and perspective embedded.
A message is also embedded (Don't touch me).
The cartoon moon, the papaya with palm tree,

the face of the figure who went to his death
with a chiseled look. What more is there? Tears
and repentance? An amaryllis turns
to say good-bye. Good-bye. Enormous sky

page. Harmony of the player/eraser unreeling.
The impeccable natural when nature reveals
its true salt.
In the heart of the morning,

the evening. The ten o'clock window opens
and inquiry enters: Who are you?
Alice retracts what she said earlier. Says instead,
I'll only be more reckless if ever I wake.

What Moonlight Will Do for Ruins

She has a theory. It's tied to the velvet
that holds her hair back. She says, this is Time,
and undoes the ribbon. Her hair cascades.
The girl no longer believes
in change. Nothing can reclaim
the rough of worn ridge and worn crater.

Every Monday she turns over the stones,
scrapes off the tiny worms with a handflat
and transforms nada. It is stupidly given, she says,
of the hour—its thin pitch, indivisible with
the taxed heart. The longitude of terror
a conforming arc that can't be undone.

Outside the mind is fact: the sea floor seasonal
in the shallow, seasonal in the deep. Time the illusion
no more bewildering than the woolly legs,
the elastic lungs, the long tube's helly depths.
Here darling, take this
and Time gives the mouth a morsel.

The Artworks

Bruce Pearson, *Rock and Roll Is Dead, The Novel Is Dead, God Is Dead, Painting Is Dead*, acrylic on Styrofoam, 2003

David Lynch, *Mulholland Drive*, feature film, color, written and directed by David Lynch, starring Naomi Watts and Laura Harring, 2001

Neo Rauch, *Takt* (Tact), oil on canvas, 1999

Michael Van Hook, *Three Trees*, oil on canvas, 1998

Lisa Cholodenko, *High Art*, feature film, written and directed by Lisa Cholodenko, starring Ally Sheedy, Radha Mitchell, and Patricia Clarkson, 1998

Sigmar Polke, Illus. 3, essay: "Early Influences, Later Consequences or: *How Did the Monkeys Get into My Work?* and other icono-biographical questions" (trans. from the German by John S. Southard), in *The Three Lies of Painting*, Sigmar Polke, Cantz Press, 1996

Sigmar Polke, *Die drei Lü gen der Malerei* (The Three Lies of Painting), synthetic resin on polyester fabric, partially printed, 1994

Sigmar Polke, *Rokoko II* (Rococo II), acrylic on canvas, 1994

Doris Salcedo, *Atrabiliarios* (Melancholy), wall installation with ten niches and eleven boxes: drywall, shoes, cow bladder, and surgical thread, 1992–3

Gilbert and George, *The Singing Sculpture*, video of performance piece, produced and directed by Philip Haas, 1992

Sigmar Polke, *Laterna Magica* (*Die Geschichte vom Hund*), [Laterna Magica (The Story of the Dog)], various lacquers on transparent polyester fabric, painted on both sides, seven sections, 1988–92

Sigmar Polke, *Frau Herbst und ihre zwei Tochter* (Mrs. Autumn and Her Two Daughters), synthetic resin on polyester fabric, 1991

Damien Hirst, *The Physical Impossibility of Death in the Mind of Someone Living*, tiger shark in a glass tank of formaldehyde, 1991

Felix Gonzalez-Torres, *Untitled* (*The End*), offset prints on paper, 1990

Ken Warneke, *The Tyranny of Everyday Life*, oil and acrylic on Masonite, 1990

Sigmar Polke, *Jeux d'enfants* (Children's Games), synthetic resin and dispersion on fabric, 1988

Paula Rego, *In the Garden*, acrylic on paper on canvas, 1986

Shiro Kuramata, *How High the Moon Chairs,* brushed aluminum chairs, 1986

Robert Gober, *Three Parts of an X,* plaster, wood, steel, wire, lath, and paint, 1985

Sigmar Polke, *Neid und Habgier II* (Envy and Avarice II), lacquer on canvas, 1985

Sigmar Polke, *Flechen* (Spots), oil on fabric, 1984

Dorothea Tanning, *Etched Murmurs,* etching, 1984

Victor Burgin, *The Bridge,* detail, black-and-white photo-construction, 1984

Sigmar Polke, *Katastrophentheorie IV* (Catastrophe Theory IV), synthetic and natural resin on canvas, 1983

Sigmar Polke, *Katastrophentheorie III* (Catastrophe Theory III), synthetic and natural resin on canvas, 1983

Sigmar Polke, *Katastrophentheorie II* (Catastrophe Theory II), synthetic and natural resin on canvas, 1983

Sigmar Polke, *So sitzen Sie richtig (nach Goya)* [This Is How You Sit Correctly (after Goya)], acrylic on fabric, 1983

Paula Rego, *Going Out,* acrylic on paper, 1982

Sigmar Polke, *Das war schon immer so* (It's Always Been Like This), pigment in synthetic resin sealer on burlap, 1982

Cindy Sherman, *Untitled #70,* color photograph, 1980

Derek Jarman, *The Tempest,* written by William Shakespeare, directed by Derek Jarman, (in which Elizabeth Welch sings "Stormy Weather"), starring Heathcote Williams and Toyah Willcox, 1979

Philip Guston, *Allegory,* oil on canvas, 1975

Sigmar Polke, *Blauer Gedankenkreis* (Blue Thought Circle), lacquer on canvas, 1974

Jean Dubuffet, *Paysage cursif* (Cursive Landscape), colored crayons and felt-tip pen on paper, 1974

Sigmar Polke, *Alice im Wunderland* (Alice in Wonderland), mixed media on patterned fabric, 1971

Willem de Kooning, *Minnie Mouse,* oil on canvas, 1971

Sigmar Polke, *Liebesparr* (Lovers), lacquer and ballpoint pen on canvas, 1967

Sigmar Polke, *Puppe* (Doll), acrylic on canvas, 1965

Jasper Johns, *In Memory of My Feelings—Frank O'Hara*, oil on canvas with objects, 1961

Eikoh Hosoe, No. 24 from the *Man and Woman* series, black-and-white photograph, 1960

Ad Reinhardt, *Abstract Painting, Blue*, oil on canvas, 1952

Francis Bacon, *Study for a Portrait*, oil on Canvas, 1949

Max Beckmann, *Masquerade*, oil on canvas, 1948

Irving Penn, *Max Ernst and Dorothea Tanning*, black-and-white photograph, 1947

Dorothea Tanning, *Birthday*, oil on canvas, 1942

Salvador Dalí, *The Phenomenon of Ecstasy*, photomontage, 1933

Margaret Bourke-White, *Machine Dance: Moscow Ballet School*, black-and-white photograph, 1931

Max Ernst and Hans Arp, *Physiomythological Diluvian Picture*, collage, 1920

Pablo Picasso, *Les Demoiselles d'Avignon*, oil on canvas, 1907

Odilon Redon, *L'oeil, comme un ballon bizarre se dirige vers l'Infini* (The Eye Like a Strange Balloon Mounts Toward Infinity), charcoal on paper, 1882

Samaria, fragment, architectural design, egg and dart motif with shadows, Roman painting, 1 BC

Mary Jo Bang, *What Moonlight Will Do for Ruins*, mixed media collage, 2003